Pearls of Purity

A Handbook for Young Ladies

read chapter 3

Kim Morrison Griggs

Dedicated to:

My two beautiful granddaughters

Miss Micaiah Ransby
Miss Ailayah Ransby

May you always walk in purity before the Lord your God; trusting
Him to ordain and orchestrate each relationship in your lives, and
may Christ the Hope of Glory be formed in you by your choice.

Contents

Acknowledgments

My Lord and Master, Jesus Christ and Holy Spirit for consistently loving, teaching, feeding, and guiding me. Thank You Lord for filling me with Your Spirit and gently blowing me into my destiny with Your Wind.

The love of my life here on earth is my darling husband, Alvin James Griggs. Thank you for propping me up! You are truly the wind beneath my wings and I love and appreciate you dearly.

My Pastor, Apostle Fritz Musser of Tabernacle International Church, who truly inspires me by his exemplary lifestyle and commitment to the Lord Jesus Christ. I am grateful to him for editing this book and gently guiding me. Thank you for laboring to feed me fresh manna weekly!

First Lady Pastor Lisa Musser, who believed in the vision God gave to me from the beginning and supported me every step of the journey. She played a participatory role in Pearls of Purity and prayed with and for me constantly.

Pastor Derresha Sailors, a humble intercessor who was prompted by Holy Spirit to ask me to teach the youth on Purity. Out of her obedience, "Pearls of Purity" was born. I am grateful for her continued support and prayers during this endeavor.

Foreword

It is such an honor to write the Foreword of Pearls of Purity for my friend, Kim Griggs. I have known Kim for many years and have had the pleasure of observing her strong leadership skills, pure heart and Biblical accuracy. Kim has a burning desire to lead girls in becoming young ladies and women of God.

Pearls of Purity was birthed out of this passion and strategically leads the reader through the process of becoming a young lady from the most practical skills of etiquette to character development and ultimately holiness (purity) and complete consecration to God. I have personally observed the way young ladies are drawn to Kim. She relates very well to them, in writing and in person, with her unique style and caring ways.

Pearls of Purity is an interactive book, ideal for teaching in a classroom setting. It is also very effective for one-on-one teaching or even as private reading for personal development. The power and presence of God is on every single page and every word of this material. It has a profound and undeniable impact on the reader. I have personally witnessed the powerful transformation of many young ladies as a direct result of Kim's teachings in this book. I highly recommend this book and Kim's wisdom and insight, more so than any other material I have ever seen on this subject.

Pastor Lisa Musser
First Lady
Tabernacle International Church
Lawrenceville, Georgia

Introduction

A "natural" pearl is one that is found in an oyster at the bottom of the ocean. There are lessons to be learned as we take a look at the oyster. For example, just as this oyster dwells at the bottom of the ocean--we must learn to posture ourselves in a low position of humility. This allows God to purify us with His Love! And He will exalt us in His timing. Imagine living at the feet of Jesus. We must grow up into maturity to handle these promotions from God. There is a great reward for exercising humility ("Going Low"). We know that Christ humbled Himself and is our Greatest Example!

Oysters have a very hard shell that protects them, but something like a small grain of sand can get inside the shell and it causes a lot of pain and discomfort for the oyster. God has given the oyster a way to ease that pain. When a grain of sand gets in there, the oyster releases a liquid called "nacre" that coats the grain of sand and then it hardens. The oyster keeps doing this over and over until the grain of sand no longer causes pain. This is the process of how these pearls are formed. Something that started out being painful turned into something very *beautiful* and *valuable*. This same process happens to us. Many times trials come into our lives that cause a lot of hurt and pain. When that happens, God gives us something to help ease the pain. He gives us His love. When we earnestly come to Him asking for help—He will release His Unconditional Love to ease our pain and suffering.

Similarly as with the oyster...what started out to be very painful in our lives can turn into something very *beautiful* and *valuable*! God is always waiting with open arms to embrace us and to see us through this process of maturing. Trials come to make us stronger and better...not weaker and bitter. Oh that we would grasp this concept: that the Lord is our Helper and wants us to offer ourselves to Him willingly; that our lives may be fragrant with Him and Him only.

The age of eleven through eighteen is very difficult for boys as well as girls. However, some say that it is a more challenging season for girls. We believe that these girls are precious to God and He wants to use them for His Glory in these last days! Yes, this stage of life can also be very painful and discomforting for girls. They are experiencing physical and emotional changes, peer pressure, and relationship issues. Some even struggle with eating disorders, acne, and weight control. These are just a few examples; but our God is able to raise them up and sustain them through His Spirit and the power of His Word in Jesus' name!

My Pastor, Apostle Fritz Musser, delivered a powerful message that inspired me! He spoke about us identifying who we are in Christ Jesus. This is an endeavor we should all practice regularly. More importantly, I heard a cry from his message for us to allow Christ in us to be formed according to Galatians 4:19. Just as the piece of sand is being formed into a pearl inside the oyster; so Christ is a Pearl of a Great Price inside us longing to be formed.

Another name for the "nacre" solution is "Mother of Pearl." This is so fitting since it covers the sand to form the pearl. And Jesus is our mother; father, brother, sister, confidant and so much more. His Love poured out in us will cause us to be just like Him. He was the Father's only begotten Son...yet He gave Him to redeem a lost and dying world. This is why a girl's virginity is priceless!!! She is valued as an extremely expensive, unique gem to God and her Parents. It is imperative that we understand the importance and urgency of Salvation. Once Jesus enters into her heart, He can begin to be formed inside her. Having pre-marital sex could damage a girl's life and she does not even realize it has happened. Can you imagine wearing a soft pearl? Of course not—pearls have to be hardened! The longer that sand/pearl stays inside that oyster shell, the harder and more beautiful it gets! Our girls must treasure and protect their virginity until they are married. As long as Jesus Christ is living inside these girls and they are allowing Him to be formed—He will keep them and bring them into maturity! Staying pure and keeping your "Purity Ring" on your finger until your fiancée places the engagement ring on is impossible without Jesus Christ!

A lady's wedding night should be very pure and holy. So young ladies...I beseech you to accept Jesus' invitation to be formed inside of you until you too have been hardened (matured) just as the pearl inside the oyster. Remember to keep your virginity wrapped inside its beautiful gift until God sends your husband into your life to unwrap you.

Chapter One

PURITY

When the word "Purity" is mentioned, most people think of clean, white, chaste, and virginity. While these are all true, there is still a need and a cry from our youth on "How to walk in Purity?" This is not an easy endeavor and it is only achievable through Christ Jesus. As young ladies, you must offer determination, submission, willingness, and tenacity.

What is Purity?

Vine's defines it as the chastity, which excludes all impurity of spirit, manner, or act.

Webster defines it as the quality or state of being pure: freedom from impurities, freedom from guilt or sin

Our foundational Scripture is found in 1 Timothy 4:12 and this is the New International Version:

"Don't let anyone look down on you because you are young, but set an example for the believers in speech, in conduct, in love, in faith and in purity."

In this Scripture "Speech" is listed first. However, I believe that we should start with "Purity" and work our way backward. When I think of purity—I can't help but think of Mary the mother of Jesus. She had to be chosen because of purity. God would not have it any other way. Many believe that Mary was between 14-16 years old.

It was a custom in the Jewish community for a girl to get engaged and later marry at this age. An engagement or betrothal during Mary's time could be as long as a year. **But we live in America and do not believe in allowing our daughters to get engaged at the age of 14 years old.** That is one of the purposes of this teaching—to help you deal with the changes that are happening in your body right now. We will share more about this later.

Let's look at the Scriptures of Mary's account in the King James Version of the Bible in Luke 1:26-38

> *26 And in the sixth month the angel Gabriel was sent from God unto a city of Galilee, named Nazareth,*
> *27 To a virgin espoused to a man whose name was Joseph, of the house of David; and the virgin's name was Mary.*
> *28 And the angel came in unto her, and said, Hail, thou that art highly favoured, the Lord is with thee: blessed art thou among women.*
> *29 And when she saw him, she was troubled at his saying, and cast in her mind what manner of salutation this should be.*
> *30 And the angel said unto her, Fear not, Mary: for thou hast found favour with God.*
> *31 And, behold, thou shalt conceive in thy womb, and bring forth a son, and shalt call his name Jesus.*
> *32 He shall be great, and shall be called the Son of the Highest: and the Lord God shall give unto him the throne of his father David.*

*33 And he shall reign over the house of Jacob
for ever; and of his kingdom there shall be no
end.
34 Then said Mary unto the angel, How shall
this be, seeing I know not a man?
35 And the angel answered and said unto her,
The Holy Ghost shall come upon thee, and the
power of the Highest shall overshadow thee:
therefore also that holy thing which shall be
born of thee shall be called the Son of God.
36 And, behold, thy cousin Elisabeth, she hath
also conceived a son in her old age: and this is
the sixth month with her, who was called barren.
37 For with God nothing shall be impossible.
38 And Mary said, Behold the handmaid of the
Lord; be it unto me according to thy word. And
the angel departed from her.*

And then the angel left her. Can you imagine that
happening to you? An angel appearing to you and
saying…in John W. Schoenheit's words, "You are gonna
give birth to the Promised Messiah." She wanted to know
how in the world could it happen because Mary was a
virgin. Look again at verse 35,

*35 And the angel answered and said unto her,
The Holy Ghost shall come upon thee, and the
power of the Highest shall overshadow thee:
therefore also that holy thing which shall be
born of thee shall be called the Son of God.*

The angel referred to Jesus as "Holy Thing" You cannot
talk about Purity without mentioning holy. And we will
discuss holiness later on in the book.

I believe the Holy Spirit wants to overshadow you all and equip you with the power to overcome obstacles that would come your way. Do you believe the Holy Spirit can give you the power to stay pure?

Write your answer here. _____ Yes _____ No

Below write our foundational Scripture. You will need to memorize this. Be sure to include the reference.

_____

_____

_____

_____

_____

_____

_____

_____

_____

You are a gift of God and very PRICELESS! Say it with me, "I am Priceless!" God has given you many words to describe you:

Priceless	Valuable
Precious	Holy
Peculiar	Powerful
Pretty	Beautiful
Pearl	Strong
Princess	Wise

Can you think of any more words? Write them below:

Jewl, Passionate, Fearless,
Spirited, Gentle, Caring,
Intelligent

In Genesis when God created mankind...this is what He said:

> *"And God saw everything that He had made, and behold, it was very good (suitable, pleasant) and he approved it completely." Gen. 1:31a (AMP)*

I don't care what anyone has said to you, here is what the Word of God says about you. He created you very good, suitable, and pleasant and He approves you COMPLETELY!

If your parents, aunts, uncles, teachers, or friends have called you names or told you..."you are ugly," you have to forgive them and move on! Would you believe that your virginity is Holy to the Lord! Sex is a Holy Thing between a married man and woman.

Points to Ponder...

- What does Purity mean?

  To be clean, holy, and free of sin

- How much am I worth?

  Priceless

15

A. Handmaid/Handmaiden of the Lord

A handmaiden of the Lord is a female servant. This refers to Mary's willingness to serve almighty God by bearing Jesus Christ in her womb. Mary was indeed a handmaiden of the Lord. By agreeing to be His servant meant that she would submit to whatever He wanted. I believe that Mary was full of humility. Ultimately, she became the mother of the Savior of the world!

Accept that it is okay to "Go Low" i.e. Be Humble. Jesus is our example and He was extremely **Humble**!!!

Proverbs 18:12 says:

> *"Haughtiness goes before destruction; humility precedes honor."*

As you humble yourself there are four choices to be made.

Submit   _____

Serve   ____✓____

Succumb   _____

Surrender   _____

Put a check on the line next to the one you are willing to do.

16

Remember: When you do all these it is not for people. Look at this Scripture in Colossians 3:17 (AMP).

"And whatever you do [no matter what it is] in word or deed, do everything in the name of the Lord Jesus and in [dependence upon] His Person, giving praise to God the Father through Him."

Notice it does not read, "Do it for your parents" or "Do it for your teachers." Nor does it read, "Do it for your Pastor!" No, you do it in the name of Jesus. Why?

_____

_____

_____

Yes, because you love Him and He gave Himself for you. We also desire to please the Lord. Allow the Lord to promote you when He says you are ready. This is exactly what happened to Mary. What a promotion? Think about this:

The Holy Spirit overshadowed Mary and planted the Incorruptible Seed in her womb. Remember how a pearl is formed? When a particle of sand gets inside of the oyster it causes discomfort. The nacre is released from the oyster several times a day and coats that particle over and over again. The more nacre—the larger and harder the particle becomes.

Finally, at the right time a pearl is formed. Many times there are discomforts during those nine months. And when it is time to give birth—there is much pain! Jesus was being formed on the inside of Mary. Imagine that…the PEARL of a Great Price right there growing inside her body. What a sacrifice…Thank you Mary for being willing to endure discomfort to bring our Savior into the world.

(I believe that Mary may have experienced some social discomfort as well. Can you imagine how she would have felt if they had Facebook or Instagram in those days?)

In those days a lady would be stoned to death for becoming pregnant before marriage. Joseph and Mary were already engaged. Also, the Lord visited Joseph in a dream to assure him that Mary's conception was of the Spirit and not by another man.

Handmaidens of the Lord

Mary the Virgin Mother: (KJV)

Luke 1:38 And Mary said, Behold the handmaid of the Lord; be it unto me according to thy word. And the angel departed from her.

Esther: (Purim) (KJV)

Esther 2:7 And he brought up Hadassah, that is, Esther, his uncle's daughter: for she had neither father nor mother, and the maid was fair and beautiful; whom Mordecai, when her father and mother were dead, took for his own daughter.

8 So it came to pass, when the king's commandment and his decree was heard, and when many maidens were gathered together unto Shushan the palace, to the custody of Hegai, that Esther was brought also unto the king's house, to the custody of Hegai, keeper of the women.

9 And the maiden pleased him, and she obtained kindness of him; and he speedily gave her things for purification, with such things as belonged to her, and seven maidens, which were meet to be given her, out of the king's house: and he preferred her and her maids unto the best place of the house of the women.

Ruth: (KJV)

Ruth 2:13 Then she said, Let me find favour in thy sight, my lord; for that thou hast comforted me, and for that thou hast spoken friendly unto thine handmaid, though I be not like unto one of thine handmaidens.

Ruth 3:9 And he said, Who art thou? And she answered, I am Ruth thine handmaid: spread therefore thy skirt over thine handmaid; for thou art a near kinsman.

Hannah: (KJV)

1 Samuel 1:11 And she vowed a vow, and said, O Lord of hosts, if thou wilt indeed look on the affliction of thine handmaid, and remember me, and not forget thine handmaid, but wilt give unto thine handmaid a man child, then I will give him unto the Lord all the days of his life, and there shall no razor come upon his head.

1 Samuel 1:16 Count not thine handmaid for a daughter of Belial: for out of the abundance of my complaint and grief have I spoken hitherto.

1 Samuel 1:18 And she said, Let thine handmaid find grace in thy sight. So the woman went her way, and did eat, and her countenance was no more sad.

handwritten note at top: 1 page report
*About Mary
If it was me

Points to Ponder...

- Who is your favorite Handmaiden in the Bible?

  Mary

- Why?

  Because she was ame.

People pleaser/God pleaser

B. <u>Holiness</u> = Divine Character

Holiness does not mean putting on a white dress! Although being clean does come to mind when I think of holiness. How many have ever heard this saying, "Cleanliness is next to Godliness?" I grew up going to a "Holiness" church and it was very strict. Growing up in The Church of God in Christ church meant no makeup, no pants, and no boys for me! Times have changed, The "NO BOYS" still holds true to holiness today.

We know that God is Holy and He also asks us to be holy in 1 Peter 1:15-16

> ***"But now you must be holy in everything you do, just as God who chose you is holy. For the Scriptures say, 'You must be holy because I am holy.'"***

We cannot go to God just any way. He must be approached with the utmost reverence and respect. Think of someone whom you really have a high regard. You may be thinking of your mother, father, teacher, pastor or grandmother. Can you go to one of these persons in muddy clothes and get a kiss? Or can you cuss them out real good and then demand that they give you $50 to buy a new dress?

Are you holy? ___✓___Yes _____No

Explain why you chose yes or no below.

Because instead of only thinking of myself I also think of the part of god inside me.

We probably should also look at the word sacred when we talk about holiness. Sacred refers to being dedicated and devoted to someone or a purpose. Are you dedicated to God? When you dedicate yourself to someone or something this means, they or it has exclusive rights to you. Think about that for a moment. Who do you spend most of your time with? What do you spend most of your time doing?

Holiness in its truest sense refers to "Sanctification," and separation to God, according to Vine's. This is not a bad thing. What does "Separation to God" mean? Does it mean He wants to begin cleaning your house? Your house is your body/temple, right? When this process starts and God starts sweeping, don't be like a dust bunny trying to hide. Dust bunnies do not want to be swept up.

I realize that it may be difficult for a pre-teen or teenager to live a life separated unto God—

Sanctification starts here: Salvation ends here: Glorification

especially in school amongst your peers. In fact, this is impossible for you to do in your own strength. But you can do it with God's help...all you have to do is ask Him to help you.

Describe holiness below?

_____

_____

_____

_____

_____

Pray:

Father in the name of Jesus, I want to be holy and I realize that it is impossible without You. Forgive me for following my own ways. Help me to be clean and pure on the inside. Teach me Your ways and give me an understanding heart. Lord give me a heart to serve You daily. Thank You Lord for changing my heart. I love You...in Jesus' name. Amen.

_____

_____

_____

_____

Smith Wigglesworth said in his book, "Ever Increasing Faith."

"The Lord shall preserve thee from all evil: he shall preserve thy soul" (Psalm 121:7). How does Satan get an opening? When the saint ceases to seek after holiness, purity, righteousness, truth; when he ceases to pray, stops reading the Word and gives way to carnal appetites, then it is that Satan comes. So often sickness comes as a result of disobedience. David said, "Before I was afflicted, I went astray." Seek the Lord and He will sanctify every thought, every act, till your whole being is ablaze with holy purity and your one desire will be for Him who has created you in holiness. Oh, this holiness! Can we be made pure? We can. Every inbred sin must go. God can cleanse away every evil thought. Can we have a hatred for sin and a love for righteousness? Yes, God will create within thee a pure heart. He will take away the stony heart out of the flesh. He will sprinkle thee with clean water and thou shalt be cleansed from all thy filthiness. When will He do it? When you seek Him for such inward purity."

- Get your minds right

   Did you know that your actions are following your thoughts? Whatever you are thinking about...you will eventually do. We should be thinking about things that are pure, lovely, kind thoughts according to Philippians 4:8

   (By the way, this includes music as well. Choose appropriate music.)

"So brace up your minds; be sober (circumspect, morally alert); set your hope wholly and unchangeably on the grace (divine favor) that is coming to you when Jesus Christ (the Messiah) is revealed. [Live] as children of obedience [to God];do not conform yourselves to the evil desires [that governed you] in your former ignorance [when you did not know the requirements of the Gospel]. But as the One Who called you is holy, you yourselves also be holy in all your conduct and manner of living. For it is written, You shall be holy, for I am holy."

1 Peter 1:13-16 (AMP)

Look further down in this passage at verse 22 in the KJV:

22 Seeing ye have purified your souls in obeying the truth through the Spirit unto unfeigned love of the brethren, see that ye love one another with a pure heart fervently:

Write this verse on the lines below:

_____

_____

_____

_____

This is the way to walk in "Purity" ladies. Your soul is made up of three parts: mind, will (volition) and emotions.

The Mind...

In your mind is where the battle takes place. Your thoughts come from God, the devil and you. When you recognize an evil thought from the devil you must do 2 Corinthians 10:5 (KJV).

> ~ *Cast down imaginations and every high thing that exalts itself against the knowledge of God*

> ~ *Bring into captivity every thought to the obedience of Christ*

What does this mean? To cast means to throw. Above in 1 Peter 1:22 it reads you must obey the truth through the Spirit.

Ask Holy Spirit to help you obey 2 Corinthians 10:5. Take those evil thoughts and throw them down under your feet. For example:

> *A young lady who is on the honor roll gets attacked in her mind. The other students are saying to her, "You think you're so smart," or "Here comes Ms. Encyclopedia." She must go into the restroom (if she's at school) as soon as possible and say/pray, "Lord, I thank You for giving me wisdom, understanding and intellect.*

Thanks for helping me excel in every area of my life. I forgive _____ for being jealous of me and for speaking evil against me. Lord, help _____ to walk in love and if she doesn't know You; I pray that You would send a laborer across her path to share the Gospel with her that she may receive salvation.

You see the Bible talks about praying for our enemies. The obedience of Christ refers to doing what Jesus would have done. Also locating a Scripture to fit every evil thought and praying it out loud.

Your Will...

This involves you making a choice or decision by using your will. In other words—you agree with the thought by saying yes as you obey. Because your body will follow that decision you make. Your decisions must line up with God's Word. Do you see why it is important to know the Word of God? The truth in 1 Peter 1:22 is one in the same as the Word of God! And you cannot obey without the help of Holy Spirit. He is your companion and walks with you and also lives inside of you. Reading your Bible daily will help. Many read a chapter of Proverbs daily for wisdom.

Your Emotions...

Emotions definitely refer to feelings. When it comes to walking in "Purity" you absolutely cannot rely on your emotions. Why? Your emotions are like an elevator—they go up and down. The Word of God will keep you balanced. The Truth is solid as a rock and will never die.

You can rely on the Word of God all the time for it is steady. Look further down in 1 Peter 1:24 (KJV):

> *"For all flesh is as grass, and all the glory of man as the flower of grass. The grass withereth, and the flower thereof falleth away: But the word of the Lord endureth for ever. And this is the word which by the gospel is preached unto you."*

You may be wondering why I capitalize "Word" so much. It is because of John 1:1 (KJV):

> **"In the beginning was the Word, and the Word was with God, and the Word was God."**

This is why it is imperative that you **know** the truth. You must **know** Jesus—for He is the Truth. Once you have mastered 1 Peter 1:22a then you will be able to love everyone else. When you get your vertical act together with Jesus (by the help of Holy Spirit), then you can walk in love with your parents, siblings, friends and even your enemies.

- Live as Children of Obedience
  Romans 6:16 (KJV), "Know ye not, that to whom ye yield yourselves servants to obey, his servants ye are to whom ye obey; whether of sin unto death, or of obedience unto righteousness?"

  Colossians 3:20 (KJV), "Children, obey your parents in all things: for this is well pleasing unto the Lord."

- Dealing with Evil desires/urges
  Romans 8:13 (KJV), "For if ye live after the flesh, ye shall die: but if ye through the Spirit do mortify the deeds of the body, ye shall live."

  Colossians 3:5 (KJV), "Mortify therefore your members which are upon the earth; fornication, uncleanness, inordinate affection, evil concupiscence, and covetousness, which is idolatry:

It is a good thing to keep yourself occupied with other interests. Do you like Basketball, Softball, Skating, Bowling, Tennis, Swimming, Dancing, Exercising or Reading? This will help your body in many ways as you are developing. When you do physical activities your brain produces endorphins, i.e. "happy chemicals," into your body. The boys are playing many sports—while we don't want to get sweaty. It is okay to get sweaty—they have showers! You can still look cute in your sport clothes!

- *Psalm 24:3-5 (KJV) says, "Who shall go up into the mountain of the Lord? Or who shall stand in His Holy Place? He who has clean hands and a pure heart, who has not lifted himself up to falsehood or to what is false, nor sworn deceitfully. He shall receive the blessing from the Lord, and righteousness from the God of his salvation."*

This Scripture is a memory verse. Practice saying and writing it from the NLT version on page 62 with a friend.

Malachi 3:1-3

"Look! I am sending my messenger, and he will prepare the way before me. Then the Lord you are seeking will suddenly come to his Temple. The messenger of the covenant, whom you look for so eagerly, is surely coming," says the Lord of Heaven's Armies. But who will be able to endure it when he comes? Who will be able to stand and face him when he appears? For he will be like a blazing fire that refines metal, or like a strong soap that bleaches clothes. He will sit like a refiner of silver, burning away the dross. He will purify the so that they may once again offer acceptable sacrifices to the Lord.

Let's look at the word refine. I thought it was interesting that the Greek word for refine is *puroomai*; and it means: to burn, as of metals, burned and tried (Vine's). The word burn means to glow with heat, it is translated "fiery" in Eph. 6:16 (of the darts of the evil one). Some synonyms for burn are fiery, fire, and try.

As you can see this fire is very hot…all fire is hot! Who is sending these fiery darts described in the above reference in Ephesians 6:16? Right—Satan! Does God know all about it? Yes He does! Yet He allows it to happen. It is part of the purification process inside of you. He has given you everything you need to succeed in the word of God!

How can you protect yourself? By putting on the whole armor of God listed in Ephesians 6:10-18.

The Whole Armor of God

A final word: Be strong in the Lord and in his mighty power. Put on all of God's armor so that you will be able to stand firm against all strategies of the devil. For we are not fighting against flesh-and-blood enemies, but against evil rulers and authorities of the unseen world, against mighty powers in this dark world, and against evil spirits in the heavenly places.

Therefore, put on every piece of God's armor so you will be able to resist the enemy in the time of evil. Then after the battle you will still be standing firm. Stand your ground, putting on the belt of truth and the body armor of God's righteousness. For shoes, put on the peace that comes from the Good News so that you will be fully prepared. In addition to all of these, hold up the shield of faith to stop the fiery arrows of the devil. Put on salvation as your helmet, and take the sword of the Spirit, which is the word of God.

Pray in the Spirit at all times and on every occasion. Stay alert and be persistent in your prayers for all believers everywhere.

Putting on this armor is the same as clothing yourself with the Lord Jesus Christ? Think about the pieces carefully. Each one represents or is symbolic of Him and the completion of His Works for you and I.

You may say, "Why do I have to go through this process?" I'm so glad you asked!

A refiner's goal is to obtain "Pure Silver" from the metal. This process of extracting silver from lead is very detailed. We all have to be tried and this makes us stronger. Circumstances, challenges, situations, and conditions are coming our way to see if we can withstand the pressure. These do not come from God. The enemy wants your **FAITH**! When Satan comes to steal, kill and destroy what will you do? Will you stand on the Word and trust God during these difficult times?

If not, there will be another opportunity later. Remember the children of Israel! It took them 40 years to reach the Promised Land and that was an eleven-day journey?

Prayer:

Lord prepare me, to be a sanctuary,
Pure and holy, tried and true
and with thanksgiving,
I'll be a living, sanctuary, oh for you.

Many of you may remember this as a song. It can also be used as a prayer to God to help us to walk in purity and holiness.

In Psalms 24:3-5 (One of our memory verses) do you think God is talking about washing your hands with soap? Explain.

Chastity

Yesterday, I came downstairs for a popcorn break. My husband was watching, "Heaven Knows Mr. Allison." This movie was about a marine and an Irish nun stranded on an island in the Pacific Ocean in World War II. He was already in the middle of the movie when I arrived.

The marine (Mr. Allison) fell in love with the nun and proposed to her (Sister Angela). Mr. Allison's position was, "What if they would be the only ones on the island for years?" If this happened, Sister Angela could not take her final vows. You see when Mr. Allison proposed; Sister Angela gently turned him down. The camera zeroed in on a beautiful silver ring with hearts. She explained to Mr. Allison that she had already given her heart to Jesus!

Sister Angela continued to expound that she would get a gold ring upon taking her final vows. One reason she wears this ring is an outward showing that she belongs to Jesus Christ—his Bride! Her promise/vows consist of chastity, poverty, and obedience. I was so happy that Sister Angela remained pure during the testing period.

Now here is a play on these words, "Nun" and "None!" Please do not give the boy "*None*" of your precious, priceless gift from God! More importantly…why should he defile your body?

If he has been sleeping around with other girls he is not a virgin. You are saving your private, preciousness for someone pure also. Do you see the difference here? Do not let him contaminate you! As you know there are sexual diseases out there and you do not want to contract one…especially AIDS! I want you to know that each time a boy has sex with a girl, all of the oneness that they shared stays with him? **(By the way, it stays with the girl also.)** If you have sex with him all of it will be transmitted inside of you. I want to give you straight talk versus sweet talk. Stay pure and holy…you will not regret it. Keep trusting your Lord and Savior to keep you!

Did you know a long time ago women and men wore chastity belts to keep them from having sex?

However, people are not wearing them today. I have to admit to sometimes wanting that practice to be implemented today (Just kidding). Maybe it would help to control how often girls are getting pregnant before marriage.

Remember: One of the purposes of this class is to provide you all with tools to help you stay pure before God.

Let's look at this in Hebrews 12:5ff. I like it in KJV…

5 And ye have forgotten the exhortation which speaketh unto you as unto children, My son, despise not thou the chastening of the Lord, nor faint when thou art rebuked of him:

6 For whom the Lord loveth he chasteneth, and scourgeth every son whom he receiveth.

7 If ye endure chastening, God dealeth with you as with sons; for what son is he whom the father chasteneth not?

8 But if ye be without chastisement, whereof all are partakers, then are ye bastards, and not sons.

9 Furthermore we have had fathers of our flesh which corrected us, and we gave them reverence: shall we not much rather be in subjection unto the Father of spirits, and live?

10 For they verily for a few days chastened us after their own pleasure; but he for our profit, that we might be partakers of his holiness.

11 Now no chastening for the present seemeth to be joyous, but grievous: nevertheless afterward it yieldeth the peaceable fruit of righteousness unto them which are exercised thereby.

12 Wherefore lift up the hands which hang down, and the feeble knees;

13 And make straight paths for your feet, lest that which is lame be turned out of the way; but let it rather be healed.

14 Follow peace with all men, and holiness, without which no man shall see the Lord:

Underline the word "Holiness" and any form of "Chaste" in the passage above. How many times is it there?

_____

Points to Ponder...

Write your thoughts here.

_____

_____

_____

_____

_____

_____

_____

_____

_____

_____

Please think about making a vow/promise to the Lord about being chaste, if you have not already entered a covenant with Him.

C.   Boy Encounters

You are a gift from God, a precious pearl! Your virginity/body represents this gift. Why would you treat your "Pearl" as though it has no value? Pearls do have *Great* value. Do you realize that years ago they were worth thousands of dollars. Why? It takes years to make a precious gem. And yes, Pearls are rare. God has created each one of you unique. And He has a specific plan for each one of you. Please don't cast your Pearls to swine (Matt. 7:6). Do not believe everything you hear! Everyone is not having sex. Many boys are just bragging about having it just to make themselves look good. In fact, he will treat having sex with you like getting a trophy. He will brag about you to his friends. This is something you do want to avoid. You are not a piece of ground to conquer, ladies! You are God's Trophy! Allow God to brag on you when it is time!

You must realize if you allow a boy to unwrap your gift and you actually engage in sex; you become one with him as we mentioned earlier. Listen to me, You do not need a boy to validate you—trust your daddy.

1 Corinthians 6:15-20

> *Don't you realize that your bodies are actually parts of Christ? Should a man take his body, which is part of Christ, and join it to a prostitute? Never! And don't you realize that if a man joins himself to a prostitute, he becomes one body with her? For the Scripture say, "The two are united into one." But the person who is joined to the Lord is one spirit with him.*

———
40

Run from sexual sin! No other sin so clearly affects the body as this one does. For sexual immorality is a sin against your own body.

God is LIGHT. Can you imagine all of that coming to live inside of you? It is sad to say that this may be the reason why many do not want Him to live inside. We know that light dispels darkness and we do not want Jesus shining His flashlight on our mess. Will you make room for Him in your heart? Realizing and accepting that we do not belong to ourselves takes the stress off of our lives when we relax and let King Jesus drive.

God is also HOLY, yet HE is willing to come into your body/temple and dwell. That is so POWERFUL! We must respect HIM!

Trust Jesus to lead you and guide you.

T   Take His hand
R   Respect Him
U   Unite your heart to His heart
S   Stay with Him
T   Trust Him with your whole heart

Points to Ponder...

Do you want to be one with God or a boy? Write your thoughts here and remember this is your private book.

_____

_____

_____

_____

_____

_____

_____

_____

How can you honor God with your body?

_____

_____

_____

_____

_____

List the benefits of being one with God.

_____

_____

_____

_____

_____

Are there benefits of being one with a boy?

_____

_____

You are absolutely right. NO, not one!

Creator and Creation

You are worthy and of great value to your Creator. Get to know Him and find out why He created you. For example, if your daddy made you a dollhouse when you were little—would you go to your Doctor to ask him/her to repair it? No, because your daddy put a lot of detail in that dollhouse and he knows everything there is to know about it. While we are on this subject let me make an insert. Your friends do not know what is best for you. Often times when we are in a dilemma we run to the wrong people. God is just standing there waiting for us to come to Him as a child goes to a parent.

Establish a relationship with Jesus Christ first. I know that once you and Jesus get tight and entwined; He will give you insight to know when it is time for a husband and you are much older. Also, the Lord may even give your parent(s) a sneak peek as to who your husband will be. Trust your parents to know what is best for you. Some of their responsibilities are to protect, provide and prove some of your relationships. God gives parents insight and wisdom on how to minister to their children. God created you—He is the Creator. You and I are His creation. Why not allow yourself to be like clay in His hands—even today?

January 9

Act Like Clay [with God] Isaiah 64:8
We are the clay, and you are our potter; and we are
the work of your hand. (NKJV)

Act like clay and not like a rock. Clay has no voice of
resistance and no sound of rebellion. Clay is soft and
pliable to move, shape, and form. Clay has the hope of
change built into it. It is the picture of potential. Anything
can be done with clay. It has no limitations on it, only the
limitations of the potter. It is the voice of the potter's
heart. Clay speaks for the potter. It represents the
intentions and hopes of its potter. Clay has no permanent
flaws. In a second it can be re-made and re-created. If it
does not work, the potter can change it. It cries out
possibility. It screams adventure. It is the complete
fulfillment of the potter's life. All of His love is poured
into the clay, and all of His hope is lavished on His clay.
The potter holds nothing back. No amount of pressure,
strain, or pain can lie endured for the sake of the potter's
dream. Oh, be My clay. Stand still. Wait for My touch. It
will change you. It will form your heart and cure your
deformities. Trust MY touch. Rely on My perfect
intentions for you. You were born to be My clay, so act
like it, and I will add magnificence to your destiny as My
clay.

Taken from "Letters from God" by Ivan Tait

Make an entry in your Journal about what you have
learned in this Lesson.

But He says he loves me...

Lust is the opposite of love. That is exactly what happened in the story of Amnon and Tamar. Let's look at it in 2 Samuel Chapter 13:1-22.

1. *Now David's son Absalom had a beautiful sister named Tamar.*
2. *And Amnon, her half brother, fell desperately in love with her. Amnon became so obsessed with Tamar that he became ill. She was a virgin, and Amnon thought he could never have her.*
3. *But Amnon had a very crafty friend—his cousin Jonadab. He was the son of David's brother Shimea.*
4. *One day Jonadab said to Amnon, "What's the trouble? Why should the son of a king look so dejected morning after morning? "So Amnon told him, "I am in love with Tamar, my brother Absalom's sister."*
5. *"Well," Jonadab said, "I'll tell you what to do. Go back to bed and pretend you are ill. When your father comes to see you, ask him to let Tamar come and prepare some food for you. Tell him you'll feel better if she prepares it as you watch and feeds you with her own hands."*
6. *So Amnon lay down and pretended to be sick. And when the king came to see him, Amnon asked him, "Please let my sister Tamar come and cook my favorite dish as I watch.*
7. *Then I can eat it from her own hands."*
8. *So David agreed and sent Tamar to Amnon's house to prepare some food for him.*
9. *When Tamar arrived at Amnon's house, she went to the place where he was lying down so he*

*could watch her mix some dough. Then she
baked his favorite dish for him.*

10. *But when she set the serving tray before him, he
refused to eat. "Everyone get out of here,"
Amnon told his servants. So they all left.*

11. *Then he said to Tamar, "Now bring the food
into my bedroom and feed it to me here." So
Tamar took his favorite dish to him.*

12. *But as she was feeding him, he grabbed her and
demanded, "Come to bed with me, my darling
sister."*

13. *"No, my brother!" she cried. "Don't be foolish!
Don't do this to me! Such wicked things aren't
done in Israel.*

14. *Where could I go in my shame? And you would
be called one of the greatest fools in Israel.
Please, just speak to the king about it, and he
will let you marry me."*

15. *But Amnon wouldn't listen to her, and since he
was stronger than she was, he raped her.*

16. *Then suddenly Amnon's love turned to hate, and
he hated her even more than he had loved her.
"Get out of here!" he snarled at her.*

17. *"No, no!" Tamar cried. "Sending me away now
is worse than what you've already done to me."
But Amnon wouldn't listen to her.*

18. *He shouted for his servant and demanded,
"Throw this woman out, and lock the door
behind her!"*

19. *So the servant put her out and locked the door
behind her. She was wearing a long, beautiful
robe, as was the custom in those days for the
king's virgin daughters.*

20. *But now Tamar tore her robe and put ashes on
her head. And then, with her face in her hands,*

she went away crying.
21. *Her brother Absalom saw her and asked, "Is it true that Amnon has been with you? Well, my sister, keep quiet for now, since he's your brother. Don't you worry about it." So Tamar lived as a desolate woman in her brother Absalom's house.*
22. *When King David heard what had happened, he was very angry.*
23. *And though Absalom never spoke to Amnon about this, he hated Amnon deeply because of what he had done to his sister.*

Amnon saw someone that he wanted and took her against her will. All along he said he "loved" Tamar. When he unwrapped and tore into the inside of her gift. He manipulated her and afterwards the Bible says he hated Tamar! Wow, how can he go from loving her to hating her so fast? It was lust! Lust is deceitful and evil.

You see even if you have had sex at your free will or it was taken from you by force—you can still be pure. This is where Christ being formed inside of you comes into play. You must believe in Jesus Christ and allow Him to purify your heart and soul. There is also another element that must be a part of the purification process and that is the Word of God. The Word of God washes you each time it is read and received into your soul.

Is there someone you need to forgive for taking your virginity against your will? Or is there someone you need to forgive for forcing you to participate in any sexual act? Forgiveness sets you free in your mind so that you can move on with your life.

God desires to heal you of this hurt. This is extremely powerful and effective once you put it into action. God will take care of the person(s) who hurt you if you ask Him. It is never good to seek revenge.

"Vengeance is mine; I will repay, saith the Lord." Romans 12:19b (KJV)

Will you please pray this from a sincere heart?

Father in the name of Jesus, You said that I must forgive others. Lord, I forgive _____ for hurting me. Dear Lord, heal me of the pain I feel and purify my heart and mind. I trust You with all of my heart and will not lean on my own understanding. I believe You will take care of me from now on and I place myself in Your hands in the name of Jesus. Thank You Lord for answering my prayer.

I want you to understand the difference between Lust and Love. **Again, you do not need a man to validate you.** If your father is absent from your home, Jesus is not absent. He is present and waiting for you to ask Him to be your Father. Jesus loves you and I with an Everlasting Love.

Read these Scriptures out loud:

Romans 13:14; Galatians 5:16, 24; Ephesians 2:3; 2 Peter 2:18; 1 John 2:16

Underline the phrase "Lust of the Flesh" in your Bible.

Discussion Questions:

Could this have been avoided?

How was her conduct around boys?

Is there hope that she could ever be pure again?

Will God forgive her?

(We will talk about Conduct later on in another chapter.)

Points to Ponder...

Write in your own words the definitions of lust and love below:

Love

_____

_____

_____

_____

_____

_____

Lust

_____

_____

_____

_____

_____

_____

Chapter Two

FAITH

What is Faith?

"Faith is the confidence that what we hope for will actually happen; it gives us assurance about things we cannot see." Hebrews 11:1

Describe in your own words what faith is?

_____

_____

_____

_____

_____

_____

_____

_____

How many of you girls like to go shopping?

Great—Me too! Raise your hand if your daddy has ever given you his credit card to use. Even if it was for a moment and he was standing right next to you—raise your hand. Your name is not on the card, right? But because he is your father and has given you permission/authority to use the card—you have the power in your hand. Now, let's say your daddy has an unlimited amount of credit. Wow! Check out all this power you have right there in your hand. And when the salesperson says,

"How do you wish to pay for this?" You say, "Charge!"

When your daddy mentioned to you that it was okay to use the card and charge your items, did you believe him? Of course—your daddy would not lie to you—his Princess! So why is it so hard for us to believe that there is power in the name of Jesus? Look at Acts 3:1-11

1. *Peter and John went to the Temple one afternoon to take part in the three o'clock prayer service.*
2. *As they approached the Temple, a man lame from birth was being carried in. Each day he was put beside the Temple gate, the one called the Beautiful Gate, so he could beg from the people going into the Temple.*
3. *When he saw Peter and John about to enter, he asked them for some money.*
4. *Peter and John looked at him intently, and Peter said, "Look at us!"*
5. *The lame man looked at them eagerly, expecting some money.*
6. *But Peter said, "I don't have any silver or gold*

for you. But I'll give you what I have. In the
name of Jesus Christ the Nazarene, get up and
walk!"
7. *Then Peter took the lame man by the right hand*
   and helped him up. And as he did, the man's feet
   and ankles were instantly healed and
   strengthened.
8. *He jumped up, stood on his feet, and began to*
   walk! Then, walking, leaping, and praising God,
   he went into the Temple with them.
9. *All the people saw him walking and heard him*
   praising God.
10. *When they realized he was the lame beggar they*
    had seen so often at the Beautiful Gate, they
    were absolutely astounded!
11. *They all rushed out in amazement to Solomon's*
    Colonnade, where the man was holding tightly
    to Peter and John.

You may say, "How is this like using a credit card?"
When someone gives you credit, they are trusting you
based on your reputation among other things. Does Christ
Jesus have a good reputation? Yes, He does! Has He ever
once answered one of your prayers? Do you have any
reason not to believe Him when He says My Power is
Unlimited???

Let's use another example of Faith:

How many of you have a bank account already? For
those of you who do not have one, I want you to pretend
you do. Everyone knows how it works—you open an
account with money. Upon opening this account the bank
gives you a "Debit Card." Oh my, this is so exciting!!!

You continue to deposit money into your account. One day you decide to go shopping and see this beautiful outfit with matching shoes! All the while going up to the register—you are thinking how good you will look in these new clothes and shoes.

Okay, can we stop right here and just be honest about how we feel at this moment? I don't know about you, but at this point—I have already selected my jewelry that will pair so well with this new outfit. Need I go on? All right...back to the scenario:

When you arrive at the sales counter and pull out your debit card. The saleslady says, "I'm sorry, your card was declined."

You are wondering what is the problem. The people in the line are giving you the looks. All of a sudden you realize that you do not have enough money in your account to cover the clothes and shoes. Of course you have to put the clothes back on the rack. And you are very disappointed.

Do you know you have a "Faith Bank Account?" And you may be asking, "How can I put faith in my account?" You make deposits by speaking the word of God. Faith comes by hearing and hearing by the word of God. It is good to say it out loud so that you can hear it. Practice saying things like this:

> **"Lord, I believe the Word of God is true. I believe that You have given me faith according to Romans 12:3.**

I believe that there is power in my words. I believe that You will keep me in perfect peace as I keep my mind on You."

What have you been saying? If you have been speaking doubt—that is what you have in your account. Change your speech! The Bible does not read, "What hindered you?" It reads in Galatians 5:7, "Who?"

> *"You were running the race so well. Who has held you back from following the truth?"*

Please realize the "Who," could very well be **you**. All we have to do is believe in His name! There is POWER in the name of JESUS!

Peter gave the man what he had---what did he have?

_____

And don't forget your Father in Heaven loves you a lot more than your earthly father.

Points to Ponder...

- What is hindering me from truly believing God?

  _____

  _____

  _____

  _____

  _____

  _____

- Who is hindering me from truly believing God?

  _____

  _____

  _____

  _____

  _____

  _____

  _____

  _____

A.   Word of God

The Word of God/Scripture has much to do with Faith. In fact, look at this:

> *But what does it say? "The word is near you; it is in your mouth and in your heart," that is, the message concerning faith that we proclaim: Romans 10:8 (NIV)*

There is a direct correlation here between the mouth and heart. We will be memorizing Scripture in our next lesson. Some of you are very familiar with this. But how many of you have allowed the Word of God to move from your head to your heart? In order for Faith to work—it has to be in your heart.

You must believe what you are saying to get the word from your head to your heart. Look at the next few verses:

> *If you declare with your mouth, "Jesus is Lord," and believe in your heart that God raised him from the dead, you will be saved. For it is with your heart that you believeand are justified, and it is with your mouth that you profess your faith and are saved. As Scripture says, "Anyone who believes in him will never be put to shame." For there is no difference between Jew and Gentile—the same Lord is Lord of all and richly blesses all who call on him, for, "Everyone who calls on the name of the Lord will be saved."*

How many have confessed Jesus as your Lord? This means you had to believe a miracle—that God raised Jesus from the dead. When you received Salvation; you had to exercise your faith, right? But you have to keep flexing your muscles of faith—just as an athlete training for the Olympics trains every day! You ask, how?

1. You must build up your spirit by praying in the Spirit daily (Jude 20-21)

2. Read your Bible daily.

3. Trust God.

Above when the question was asked about confessing Jesus as your Lord—do you all understand what this means? This means that He is in charge of your life. You should be running things by Him to make sure it is okay. He really does care about every intricate detail of your life! Remember Mary? She said, "Behold the handmaid of the Lord; be it unto me according to thy word." In Luke 1:38 The New Living Translation placed the word "Servant" there. Would you prefer "Handmaid?" Make sure to check your heart attitude if you have a problem with serving.

Humility is always the way to go, so that God can exalt you when He is ready. So—GO LOW!!!

Points to Ponder...

- What have I learned in this lesson today that I can apply to my life?

_____

_____

_____

_____

_____

- What changes can I make to get the Word from my head to my heart?

_____

_____

_____

_____

Young ladies, if you do not have a belief system; someone will come along and persuade you to join in with their belief system. Be a Leader not a Follower.

B.   Scripture Memorization

How many of you can quote John 3:16?

Memorizing the Word of God is very important to your success as a Pearl of Purity. This is definitely one of the tools for you to employ. Look at what they did in the Old Testament Deut. 6:4-9,

> *"Listen, O Israel! The Lord is our God, the Lord alone. And you must love the Lord your God with all your heart, all your soul, and all your strength. And you must commit yourselves wholeheartedly to these commands that I am giving you today. Repeat them again and again to your children. Talk about them when you are at home and when you are on the road, when you are going to bed and when you are getting up. Tie them to your hands and wear them on your forehead as reminders. Write them on the doorposts of your house and on your gate."*

We are not asking you to wear the Word of God on your foreheads or tie it to your hands. However, it is very important to your success of walking in purity.

Here are Scriptures that will benefit you to memorize. These are required for you to know before participating in a Purity Ceremony.

1 Timothy 4:12 (NIV)

"Don't let anyone look down on you because you are young, but set an example for the believers, in speech, in conduct, in love, in faith, and in purity."

Psalm 24:3-5

"Who may climb the mountain of the Lord? Who may stand in his holy place? Only those whose hands and hearts are pure, who do not worship idols and never tell lies. They will receive the Lord's blessing and have a right relationship with God their savior."

Matthew 5:8

"God blesses those whose hearts are pure, for they will see God."

1 Corinthians 13

"If I could speak all the languages of earth and of angels, but didn't love others, I would only be a noisy gong or a clanging cymbal. If I had the gift of prophecy, and if I understood all of God's secret plans and possessed all knowledge, and if I had such faith that I could move mountains, but didn't love others, I would be nothing. If I gave everything I have to the poor and even sacrificed my body,

memorize from here

*I could boast about it; but if I didn't love others,
I would have gained nothing. Love is patient and
kind. Love is not jealous or boastful or proud or
rude. It does not demand its own way. It is not
irritable, and it keeps no record of being
wronged. It does not rejoice about injustice but
rejoices whenever the truth wins out. Love never
gives up, never loses faith, is always hopeful,
and endures through every circumstance.
Prophecy and speaking in unknown languages
and special knowledge will become useless. But
love will last forever! Now our knowledge is
partial and incomplete, and even the gift of
prophecy reveals only part of the whole picture!
But when the time of perfection comes, these
partial things will become useless.*

*When I was a child, I spoke and thought and
reasoned as a child. But when I grew up, I put
away childish things. Now we see things
imperfectly, like puzzling reflections in a
mirror, but then we will see everything with
perfect clarity. All that I know now is partial and
incomplete, but then I will know everything
completely, just as God now knows me
completely.*

*Three things will last forever—faith, hope, and
love—and the greatest of these is love."*

I have recited all of my Scriptures to the Teacher!

Student's Signature

_____

Teacher's Signature

_____

Note:

No student should participate in a Pearls of Purity Ceremony without memorizing the abovementioned Scriptures. The Word of God is mandatory and essential to this walk of purity.

Chapter Three

LOVE

God is Love! This is why 1 Corinthians 13 is great to get into your heart. We are commanded to Love God and one another. In fact, Jesus shared that this was the method others will know that we are His disciples. Love also should be unconditional. Remember Love gives and lust takes. If you love God with all of your heart, soul and mind; it will be easy to love everyone else.

1 John 3:1-6

> *See how very much our Father loves us, for he calls us his children, and that is what we are! But the people who belong to this world don't recognize that we are God's children because they don't know him. Dear friends, we are already God's children, but he has not yet shown us what we will be like when Christ appears. But we do know that we will be like him, for we will see him as he really is. And all who have this eager expectation will keep themselves pure, just as he is pure.*
>
> *Everyone who sins is breaking God's law, for all sin is contrary to the law of God. And you know that Jesus came to take away our sins, and there is no sin in him. Anyone who continues to live in him will not sin. But anyone who keeps on sinning does not know him or understand who he is.*

65

God's love purifies!

When you and I sincerely accepted Jesus into our hearts the sanctification process began. And we learned that this is what holiness is all about, i.e. being set apart for the Master's use. Jesus offered Himself to be crucified for us. He did not know sin, but was made to be sin that we may become the righteousness of God. This is why He is named Himself, "The Way!" Now, you and I have a way to come to the Father through the blood of Jesus Christ! That is the only way we can even pray to the Father is in Jesus' name. Isn't this Great News! See how Love gives?

Maybe this is why Paul said in Gal. 2:20:

> *My old self has been crucified with Christ. It is no longer I who live, but Christ lives in me. So I live in this earthly body by trusting in the Son of God, who loved me and gave himself for me.*

Fire purifies?

I can remember being about 12 years old and allowing my friend Sylvia to pierce my ears. I say Sylvia, but we called her Boo Boo! I had seen her ears and they looked fine and also another friend's ears. I was so nervous, but I really wanted pierced ears so I could wear earrings, right? When she burned that needle, I was petrified. The needle was being purified before entering my flesh. It did hurt— but not for long.

I had two strings hanging down from my ears for weeks. My mother was not happy. I had not received her permission and you better believe I got punished severely. During those days corporal punishment was acceptable. My mother practiced the Scripture that says, "Spare the rod...spoil the child."

In the Old Testament that is why the animals had to be sacrificed for atonement of their sins. And the priests did this by pouring out the blood and burning the animals with "Fire" on the altar. Thank God we were not living back then. Jesus shed His blood and definitely it was the Ultimate Sacrifice for us.

Look at Matthew 3:11:

> *"I baptize with water those who repent of their sins and turn to God. But someone is coming soon who is greater than I am—so much greater that I'm not worthy even to be his slave and carry his sandals. He will baptize you with the Holy Spirit and with fire.*

Why did John the Baptist say this?

_____

_____

_____

_____

_____

Listen, we need to be baptized with the Holy Spirit and fire, as it is definitely part of the sanctification *process*. And it is not a one-time deal. I ask Him to fill me each day and so should you. It is the Keeping Power of the Lord Jesus Christ!

Remember when you first moved into your home? Did you have any electrical power? If not, your parent(s) had to go to Georgia Power and pay to have your lights turned on. And if they were already on—they had to have the service placed in their name. Can you imagine living in your home without any power? Of course not! It is the same concept with Salvation.

Above it was mentioned that Jesus is a Keeper. Do you really want to be kept? If the answer is yes, then read on...Psalm 121

> *"I look up to the mountains—does my help come from there? My help comes from the Lord, who made heaven and earth! He will not let you stumble; the one who watches over you will not slumber. Indeed, he who watches over Israel, never slumbers or sleeps. The Lord himself watches over you! The Lord stands beside you as your protective shade. The sun will not harm you by day, nor the moon at night. The Lord keeps you from all harm and watches over your life. The Lord keeps watch over you as you come and go, both now and forever."*

Write your favorite part in your journal of this lesson.

A.   Pearls

I want to show you why I believe that this Pearl written below refers to our Jesus! Notice in verse 46, it mentions "A Pearl" was discovered and was of great value. Jesus is that Pearl. He was His Father's only begotten Son and the Father gave Him up because of His great love for us. Also in John 10:7, Jesus said,

> *"I am the gate for the sheep."*

Matthew 13:45-46 (KJV)

> *Again, the Kingdom of Heaven is like a merchant on the lookout for choice pearls. When he discovered a pearl of great value, he sold everything he owned and bought it!*

Revelation 21:21

> *The twelve gates were made of pearls—each gate from a single pearl! And the main street was pure gold, as clear as glass.*

Above in Matthew the merchant sold everything he owned. It cost God everything and He feels we are worth it! Remember when Abraham was willing to give up his only son? I love the part where he indicated that God would provide the Lamb for the sacrifice.

(This is when the name Jehovah Jireh, [*The Lord will provide*] was manifested.) And He did provide His only begotten Son, Jesus Christ!

At church last night we were singing, "Here I am to Worship." At around 5:00 o'clock this morning, I kept hearing:

"I'll never know,
how much it cost,
to see my sin,
up on that cross."

Young ladies, it was **LOVE** that motivated Jesus to the cross and **LOVE** that held Him on that cross! You already know John 3:16 shares just how much God loves us. How much do we love Him? We can give Him our time, talent, and treasure. Are you willing to give your time to the Lord? There are so many methods of serving and thinking of others. You are not too young to get started in serving Christ.

There was a king in the Bible who was only 8 years old when he reigned! The Scripture mentions us not despising our youth, but be an example. Look for opportunities to minister to others—even with your smile.

List ways you can serve God below:

_____

_____

_____

_____

_____

_____

_____

_____

_____

_____

_____

_____

B.   Outreach

Imagine a glass of water sitting in front of you. It looks really pure, right? Is it really pure? Did you know that if you live in Metropolitan Atlanta, you probably are drinking water from the Chattahoochee River? You may be thinking about the different particles and living creatures that live in the river. There is a water purification process that most cities have in place to purify it before we drink it.

Water purification is the process of removing undesirable chemicals, biological contaminants, suspended solids and gases from contaminated water. The goal is to produce water fit for a specific purpose. Most water is purified for human consumption (drinking water), but water purification may also be designed for a variety of other purposes, including meeting the requirements of medical, pharmacological, chemical and industrial applications. In general the methods used include physical processes such as filtration, sedimentation, and distillation, biological processes such as slow sand filters or biologically active carbon, chemical processes such as flocculation and chlorination and the use of electromagnetic radiation such as ultraviolet light. *(Taken from Wikipedia)*

It is sad to think about the fact that some countries do not have this purification system in place. They bathe and drink from the same water.

Take a moment or two to write a thank you note to God for providing clean and pure water for you to drink from your faucet:

_____

_____

_____

_____

_____

There are many Christians who are persecuted for believing in Jesus Christ. When a mother/father or both are taken away from the children, they become orphans. At this time, I would like for you to write a letter to one of these orphans. These children would love to hear that someone else is thinking of them. This section of the handbook is about Love and Love gives and reaches out to others.

The Voice of the Martyrs is a non-profit organization that serves persecuted Christians around the world since 1967. These Christians are persecuted because of their faith in Jesus Christ. Please have your instructor or your mother help you research this organization.

You may also help out in your community and church. There are so many people less fortunate than we are. We should look for opportunities to help and not just during the Christmas season.

Are you depressed and feeling sorry for yourself? It sounds strange to reach out when you feel so down; but it works! This is a great way for your heart to gain weight. Your heart grows so much as you help other people. Unlike food—you can never **do** too much for others. You do not have to wait on anyone to start a Team—start a Team of your own. Keep it pure and remember that there is no "I" in the word Team. Do not make it all about you.

You may also help out in your community and church. There are so many people less fortunate than you and I. We should look for opportunities to help and not just during the Christmas season.

Chapter Four

CONDUCT

In our foundational Scripture 1 Timothy 4:12 conduct is mentioned. Conduct refers to the way one behaves and lives. It also involves manners and the way you act socially. Many times you are the only Bible others will read. People are watching what you do as opposed to what you say. In some cultures this is the way you win others to Christ.

A.   Behavior

Body Language: As a teenager this language is used daily without you even recognizing the behavior. As parents we realize that you are still in the process of developing on many levels. There are *stages of development* that one must go through. However, I do not wish to bore my readers with them. You may choose to research these on your own.

Do you know that you can say a lot just by the way you walk? You even send different messages by the way you hold your arms? When you are upset and you fold your arms it sends out a signal that you are not letting anyone inside. You have built a wall up and around you. Let us not forget about the way you look at others sometimes.

Edward G. Wertheim, Ph.D., gives this information on non-verbal communication:

"Nonverbal communication, or body language, is a vital form of communication. When we interact with others, we continuously give and receive countless wordless signals. All of our nonverbal behaviors—the gestures we make, the way we sit, how fast or how loud we talk, how close we stand, how much eye contact we make—send strong messages."

You can order your behavior. In fact, you are the only one who can. Making a conscious effort and the decision to change can achieve this. It takes twenty-one days to form a new habit. I believe it takes twenty-one more to solidify the change.

Above we spoke about focusing on your inner-self. We do not spend enough time on the inner-life. This has a much to do with the way we behave. Our thoughts transfers to what we say and then we begin to act it out. So you wind up acting out what started out as your thoughts.

The Holy Spirit is just waiting for you to ask Him to assist you. He wants you to acknowledge Him even in your behavior and conduct. Do you want to please Him?

Look at this Prayer in Ephesians 3:14-21 on Inner Growth.

When I think of all this, I fall to my knees and pray to the Father, the Creator of everything in heaven and on earth. I pray that from his glorious, unlimited resources he will empower you with inner strength through his Spirit. Then Christ will make his home in your hearts as you trust in him. Your roots will grow down into

God's love and keep you strong. And may you have the power to understand, as all God's people should, how wide, how long, how high, and how deep his love is. May you experience the love of Christ, though it is too great to understand fully. Then you will be made complete with all the fullness of life and power that comes from God.

Now all glory to God, who is able, through his mighty power at work within us, to accomplish infinitely more than we might ask or think. Glory to him in the church and in Christ Jesus through all generations forever and ever! Amen.

You and I represent Christ Jesus as long as we are in this world. How would Jesus want you to behave? You are also a reflection of your parents everywhere you go. What if your future husband was watching you from a distance? Believe it or not boys are also being taught on holiness and how to choose the girl they want to marry by their parents and leaders at church. Make wise decisions!

Do you behave different at home/school? Explain your answer below:

_____

_____

_____

_____

Why?

_____

_____

_____

_____

_____

_____

_____

Did you know the way you dress can alter your behavior? I taught in Christian Schools for about three years and the students wore uniforms. On the days they had free dress their behaviors changed. As a young lady, a princess of Christ…you must carry yourself very well. This includes choosing the correct and appropriate clothing to represent holiness. Dressing modestly is a must and you can do it without looking like you are out of style.

B. Modesty

Modesty involves behavior, manners and the way you dress. When you think of the word "Moderate" what comes to mind? For me it means not too little and not too much. Thus, one must find a happy medium. As a young lady, choosing the appropriate clothing is imperative to walking in Purity.

1 Timothy 2:9

> **And I want women to be modest in their appearance. They should wear decent and appropriate clothing and not draw attention to themselves by the way they fix their hair or by wearing gold or pearls or expensive clothes.**

Paul is not saying don't wear jewelry here; but rather, do not let the jewelry be the focus point on your body. In other words, you should not look like Mr. "T" when you leave your home. You will draw the wrong kind of attention and attraction. When it comes to fashion please choose *modesty*.

How much time do you spend getting dressed completely? I know it is an astronomical amount of time compared to a boy, right? Look at this picture of a girl improperly dressed.

What kind of signals do you think she is sending out to boys?

_____

_____

_____

_____

Why do you think she chose this dress?

_____

_____

_____

_____

Remember earlier in the book where we talked about you as being a gift from God? You are indeed a peculiar, precious gift and you represent Him. If you choose to wear a dress like this one, the boy doesn't have to guess what is in your gift. We must be careful not to put our bodies on display with the clothes we choose to wear.

What about the clothes **you** wear? All girls do not want to dress inappropriately. We need more clothing stores who are willing to accommodate Christian young ladies. In an ABC News article written by Katie Ramly, a student said,

"I feel more comfortable with myself when I'm dressed more modestly," said Lisa Prince, one of the student shoppers. "It's been really hard for me to go school-clothes shopping or shopping in general. I just want to have more of a selection."

Young ladies are wondering why boys are trying to get their attention. Many times it is the way you dress. It is your responsibility to dress modestly to avoid this kind of encounter. If you have been dressing inappropriately, you must repent and turn from this misbehavior and get back on track!

Let's look at this scenario:

Two girls are walking down the street. One has on tight fitting clothes and the other has on modest clothing. The boy looks at both of them. Which one do you think he feels he can hit a home run with? I'm not saying dress up like a nun; but cover yourself up nicely.

This is achievable! Here is an example of a girl covered:

This is a modest outfit for a teenager. When this young lady turn around; you will not see the outline of her rear end.

C. Etiquette

This word refers to being polite and behaving correctly.
We live in a society where certain things are prohibited.
There are things that boys can do that girls just cannot get
away with. Girls have to sit a different way than boys.
Our knees must always be together. Our posture is
important. We should not ever slouch down in our chairs.
Being ladylike seems as if it has gone out of style. Young
ladies it is very attractive to have great etiquette. I believe
that it is still worth the investment to learn how to walk
confidently, set a proper table, use proper telephone
manners, show respect to elders, sit properly, and know
how to make introductions, etc. Setting a proper table is
one we will focus on in this book. Here is a picture of an
informal place setting:

I can remember going on a Field Trip to a
restaurant called Donn Clendenon's on Martin Luther
King, Jr. Drive (formerly Hunter Street) in Atlanta,
Georgia. We had to practice what we learned in the
classroom. The boys pulled out the girl's chair. We had a
Three Course Lunch and had to place our cloth napkins
on our laps correctly. We also had to use the correct
silverware. It was fun and I was hooked from then to
now.

To this day I still like eating at restaurants that have tablecloths and real napkins. Of course we had Fried Chicken and all the trimmings. There are many areas of etiquette for example, telephone, table manners, email, business, and many more. I encourage you to research further to learn these disciplines and apply them as necessary.

Another part of etiquette is **posture**. Have you ever had to walk with a book on your head? It is a good way to practice posture. Be sure to use a hardback book. Walk about nine feet to sit in a chair. Once you arrive cross your legs at the ankles to one side. Then arise confidently and walk back to starting position.

It is not appropiate to slouch in your seat or when you are standing. You never know who is watching you. Don't you want to be a role model for little girls?

Take a look at our First Lady Michelle Obama. Here knees are touching and her legs are crossed at the ankles.

Basic Etiquette varies with many people and sources. Some of these we can remember learning in Elementary School. Here is my list:

1. Basic Politeness – Practice what your parents taught you. Say, "Please" when appropriate and "Thank you." Also, do not forget to say, "You're Welcome." Remember to cover your cough to prevent spreading germs.
2. Be on Time – Ladies, please practice this one, as it will be so necessary as you get older. It is rude to be late!
3. Do not groom yourself in public – It not cool to adjust your slip, bra or panties in public. This one is self-explanatory.

4. Turn you ringer off – Do not text, check email or play games while in church. Also while at graduations, during dinner with your parents and at school.
5. Conduct polite conversation – Even if you do not agree with a person, there is no need to cause a scene or a Great Debate!

Chapter Five

SPEECH

Speech refers to speaking, sounds, and words and thoughts from the heart. Many times we speak before even thinking about what we really want to articulate or say. Words are extremely powerful and can have a long lasting affect on the person who hears them. One never knows how the recipient of words spoken will be received. Each person processes information in a different manner. Some are more sensitive than others and take words very seriously; especially from someone they respect. Please think about making a commitment to watch what you say. Perhaps you may want to go a step further and dedicate your *mouth* to the Lord.

Have you ever heard of this saying, "Sticks and stones may break by bones, but words will never hurt me?" This is so not true—words can and do hurt. Many people were hurt by words spoken to them during their adolescent years. Some of these people have never recovered and others have had to receive therapy. Kids are just having fun or showing off, but at whose expense? Make sure the words you choose are faith-filled and full of life! Your goal should be to build others up by using encouragement. Jesus encouraged us to do unto others, as you would have them do to you.

A.   Communication

Communication involves two persons. I remember as a child, making a communication device. We did not have our own walkie-talkies, so we made ours. My sister and I took two cans and attached a very long string to the end of each can and had fun playing. We were just talking and even speaking simultaneously—at the same time. Truthfully, we were not communicating. Correct communication requires two people and when one person speaks the other listens. Think about the conversations you have on the telephone with one of your friends. When you have something very exciting to share with her you really want her attention. If she does not quiet down and stop talking, you say, "Listen," or "Be Quiet I have something to say." If she still refuses to stop speaking, you may decide to quiet down and listen to her (God forbid you hang up on her). The point is—one must listen while the other speaks. If this is not done—you have no communication.

Above we mentioned how important our words are when we communicate. There is life and death in our words spoken, according to Proverbs 18:21. Watch what you say! What are you saying? The Word of God says, "You have what you say." in Mark 11:23

"Let your conversation be gracious and attractive so that you will have the right response for everyone. " Col 4:6

88

If you have suffered from verbal abuse, please make the decision to forgive that person. Even if it was one of your parents...please forgive them. It is not okay to tear others down with our words. If you are not ministering grace to the hearer—then you should keep your mouth closed. My mother used to tell us, "If you do not have anything good to say, do not open your mouth." This was good advice and I have to admit that I did not always remember to follow it. Also when we were growing up if you said bad words, parents would wash our mouths out with soap. Oh to be back in the good old days!

Why not use your mouth to praise God? Start singing to the Lord and I know He would absolutely love it. Also, it is a good thing to read the word of God out loud!

Write a little prayer below asking God to help you with words:

_____

_____

_____

_____

_____

_____

_____

_____

B. Prayer

Prayer is the key to **communication** with God! I know
you must be wondering why is prayer here in this
section. As stated above, it is communication and this
involves speaking. You know that communication
involves two people. So many forget this is true as it
relates to prayer. How many of us get up and leave our
secret place after we have asked God for what we
want? This is so unfair to God! What if He has
something to say to us? Waiting is not easy and most
people do not like to wait.

It is a practice we should employ when it comes to
getting to know our Creator.

Reasons why we may not talk to God...

There are many reasons why we do not talk to God.
We do not have to have our thee's and thou's correct.
However, we must realize that He is Holy and requires
much respect. Reverence for God is not practiced
enough, especially in His house. He is our Heavenly
Father and deserves reverence. If the President of the
United States were to come to your home for dinner,
would you treat him like one of your friends? I don't
think so! You would pull out the china and best
tablecloth and treat him like a king! God is more
important than President Barack Obama every day of
the week.

Another reason is, we are practicing sin on a regular basis in our lives. Did you know that He couldn't participate or have anything to do with sin? God will hide His face from us. Let's look at two kings and their communication with God.

The first one is King David in 2 Samuel chapter eleven:

1. In the spring of the year, when kings normally go out to war, David sent Joab and the Israelite army to fight the Ammonites. They destroyed the Ammonite army and laid siege to the city of Rabbah. However, David stayed behind in Jerusalem.

2. Late one afternoon, after his midday rest, David got out of bed and was walking on the roof of the palace. As he looked out over the city, he noticed a woman of unusual beauty taking a bath.

3. He sent someone to find out who she was, and he was told, "She is Bathsheba, the daughter of Eliam and the wife of Uriah the Hittite."

4. Then David sent messengers to get her; and when she came to the palace, he slept with her. She had just completed the purification rites after having her menstrual period. Then she returned home.

5. Later, when Bathsheba discovered that she was pregnant, she sent David a message, saying, "I'm pregnant."

Now David was not supposed to even be home at this time of year. It can be very dangerous to not be where God wants you to be. The will of God is the safest place to be…(please do not forget this). David placed himself in a difficult situation where he was tempted beyond measure. Once you commit the first sin, the next one is easier. This is why it is not good to **practice** sin. David began plotting to remove Uriah from the scene to make himself happy.

Look further at verses 14-15

In the morning David wrote a letter to Joab and sent it with Uriah. In it he wrote, "Put Uriah out in front where the fighting is fiercest. Then withdraw from him so he will be struck down and die."

Wow! He committed murder and acted like a thief too by taking this man's wife. Would God hear his prayers that night? _____

verses 26-27

When Uriah's wife heard that her husband was dead, she mourned for him. After the time of mourning was over, David had her brought to his house, and she became his wife and bore him a son.

***But the thing David had done displeased the
Lord.*** (Underlining is mine.)

David even wrote these words in Psalm 66:18, "If I
regard iniquity in my heart, the Lord will not hear me."
And in another place in Psalms 69:17, "And **hide not thy
face** from **thy** servant; for I am in trouble: hear me
speedily."

What you need to know is David did repent in Psalm 51
(where he asked God to forgive him and to create in him
a clean heart). David paid a very high price for his sin.
The son that Bathsheba gave birth to did not live. God is
so merciful that He allowed them to have another son
named Solomon.

The other King is Jesus! Jesus came to reconcile us back
to God the Father. He is the mediator between us and the
Father in Heaven.

1 John 2:2

*He himself is the sacrifice that atones for our
sins—and not only our sins but the sins of all
the world.*

God cannot abide with sin! This is why Adam and Eve
had to be evicted from the Garden of Eden.

Remember when Jesus lie on the cross crying out to His
Father, "Father, why have You forsaken Me?"

For just that amount of time the Father had no communication with Jesus. All of our sins were laid upon Jesus and He was made to be sin. Look at the following verses below:

> *"For God made Christ, who never sinned, to be the offering for our sin, [a] so that we could be made right with God through Christ." 2 Corinthians 5:21*

> *"All of us, like sheep, have strayed away. We have left God's paths to follow our own. Yet the Lord laid on him the sins of us all." Isaiah 53:6*

Once Jesus gave up His spirit by death—communication was restored between the Father God and His children. Now let's look at Jesus teaching the disciples how to pray.

Jesus' teaching on Prayer…Matthew 6:5

> *"When you pray, don't be like the hypocrites who love to pray publicly on street corners and in the synagogues where everyone can see them. I tell you the truth, that is all the reward they will ever get.*

Here Jesus instructs us on improper prayer. Some like to pray to be seen by mankind, while others pray to impress others. We must remember that we are speaking directly to God and He knows the thoughts and intents of our hearts.

Thus, when we pray in this way by impressing others, we have our reward. In other words...you received your reward when you prayed or should I say played. You may have wanted to be accepted into a position or circle. What if the leadership of your church wants you to become a Prayer Leader and you are playing around with prayer. This is a dangerous way to pray...to be seen by mankind!!!

Pitfalls of Improper Prayer

- Causing the hearers to err
- Grieving the Holy Spirit
- False hopes

You do not have to keep repeating your prayer or words over and over again. Sometimes people do this for it to appear that they can pray long prayers.

Model Prayer – A.K.A "The Lord's Prayer"

In Matthew 6:6-13, Jesus gives instructions on praying. He prefaces it this way:

> ***"But when you pray, go away by yourself, shut the door behind you, and pray to your Father in private. Then your Father, who sees everything, will reward you. When you pray, don't babble on and on as people of other religions do. They think their prayers are answered merely by repeating their words again and again. Don't be like them, for your Father knows exactly what you need even before you ask him!***

Preparation Points to Remember:

- Go into your private room
- Shut the door
- Pray to your Father in secret
- Father rewards you openly

As we prepare to pray we have to remember how to come to God. When we come to Him we really have to believe that He is really the Almighty God. We also must have the right attitude. I have created a new word...Heart-titude! I strongly recommend that you put these in your heart and give yourselves regular check-ups.

Heart-titude

Luke 18:1-8

Humility

Willingness

Teachable

Faith

Persistence

Pray therefore, like this:

> ***Our Father in heaven, may your name be kept holy. May your Kingdom come soon. May your will be done on earth, as it is in heaven. Give us today the food we need, and forgive us our sins, as we have forgiven those who sin against us. And don't let us yield to temptation, but rescue us from the evil one.***

Many pray these exact words and that is okay to start here; but we must move out into deeper waters. I believe this is a model to teach us to pray. Let me show you what I mean below:

Our Father in Heaven,
This is why we say, "Father, in the name of Jesus"…Jesus said, *"In that day you will ask in my name. I am not saying that I will ask the Father on your behalf. No, the Father himself loves you because you have loved me and have believed that I came from God.*

May your name be kept holy.
This part is definitely referring to worship! The name of Jesus is to be held in high esteem. He has so many names and sometimes I call them out to Him out loud. Jehovah Shalom, Jehovah Rapha, Jehovah Jireh, Jehovah Nissi and Jehovah Rohi!

All of these are wonderful names and once you go through all of these, you find yourself in a posture of worship! He is worthy to be exalted more than any other!

May your Kingdom come soon.
We can pray these words expressing to Him that we are looking forward to the coming of our Lord Jesus Christ to get us (His bride)! Germain Copeland wrote in her book, <u>Prayers that Avail Much</u> Volume Two:
"Today, we are [even here and] now Your children; it is not yet disclosed (made clear) what we shall be [hereafter], but we know that when He comes and is manifested we shall [as God's children] resemble and be like Him, for we shall see Him just as He [really] is. You said that everyone who has this hope [resting] on Him cleanses (purifies) himself just as He is pure – chaste, undefiled, guiltless."

May your will be done on earth, as it is in heaven.
According to Germain Copeland this part is submission to His will. You have to get into the word of God to know what this is. For example:

Father in the name of Jesus I pray that Your will be done in my life as it is in Heaven. Lord, I belong to You; my spirit, soul, and body. I am glad that You chose me before the foundations of the world. Lord, I believe You have called me to be sanctified and set apart for Your use. I submit to Your will for my life. Dear Lord, help me to obey Your word today that I may please You.

Give us today the food we need,
Father, I thank you for being my Provider of food, shelter, and clothing. I know that as I seek You first all of the necessary things will be added to me. Oh Lord,

You are my portion forever. May Your word sustain me as I meditate on it day and night. Thank you for giving my parents jobs and automobiles. You are Great and greatly to be praised!

And forgive us our sins,
Here you must ask for forgiveness by confessing your sins to Him. When you do this, He is faithful and just to forgive you and to cleanse you from all unrighteousness, according 1 John 1:9. Be sure to forgive yourself.

As we have forgiven those who sin against us.
It would be horrible for you to get all the way to this part and decide you can't forgive him/her for what they did. It is imperative that you forgive. If you do not forgive, all of the rest of the prayer before this will not count.

Jesus said in Matthew 6:14-15

> *If you forgive those who sin against you, your heavenly Father will forgive you. But if you refuse to forgive others, your Father will not forgive your sins.*

And don't let us yield to temptation,
Pray to God to help you with any and all temptations. Trust Him to hear and help you. Read this one out loud from 1 Corinthians 10:13:

> *No temptation has overtaken you except what is common to mankind. And God is faithful; he will not let you be tempted beyond what you can bear.*

But when you are tempted, he will also provide a way out so that you can endure it.

But rescue us from the evil one.
Pray to your Heavenly Father to deliver you and keep you safe from Satan. You could say,

Father in the name of Jesus I thank you for giving Your angels charge over me and keeping me safe. You are my Shield, Buckler and my Fortress. Thank You for covering me with Your feathers and under Your wings I will trust.

At this point you can go into special requests, praying for others, and any other type of prayer. Do you see how this passage of Scripture can be used as a model? Can you find a prayer in the Bible that follows this model?

How often should we pray? Jesus encouraged us to always pray and do not stop. David prayed morning, noon, and night (Psalm 55) and so did Daniel. It was a good thing Daniel was a praying man and had established a relationship with God.

His God delivered him from the den of those hungry lions. We must get to know God *now*—not when we get into trouble. And certainly not wait until when we are older! Too often young people feel as though an intimate relationship with God is for their parents. Do not be deceived!

Does God hear us? Yes He does and we must believe while we are praying. Remember what we learned earlier about Faith.

Before you even received your answer to prayer—you must act as if you already have the answer. Look at this:

1 John 5:14-15

> *And we are confident that he hears us whenever we ask for anything that pleases him. And since we know he hears us when we make our requests, we also know that he will give us what we ask for.*

In Matthew 25:1-13 (NIV) there are ten virgins preparing to meet their Groom. Look for yourself in this story:

1. *At that time the kingdom of heaven will be like ten virgins who took their lamps and went out to meet the bridegroom.*
2. *Five of them were foolish and five were wise.*
3. *The foolish ones took their lamps but did not take any oil with them.*
4. *The wise ones, however, took oil in jars along with their lamps.*
5. *The bridegroom was a long time in coming, and they all became drowsy and fell asleep.*
6. *At midnight the cry rang out: 'Here's the bridegroom! Come out to meet him!'*
7. *Then all the virgins woke up and trimmed their lamps.*
8. *The foolish ones said to the wise, 'Give us some of your oil; our lamps are going out.'*
9. *'No,' they replied, 'there may not be enough for both us and you. Instead, go to those who sell oil and buy some for yourselves.'*
10. *But while they were on their way to buy the oil,*

the bridegroom arrived. The virgins who were ready went in with him to the wedding banquet. And the door was shut.
11. *Later the others also came. 'Lord, Lord,' they said, 'open the door for us!'*
12. *But he replied, 'Truly I tell you, I don't know you.'*
13. *Therefore keep watch, because you do not know the day or the hour.*

The process of trimming a wick can be analogous to prayer. If you are not praying...you do not have any oil for your lamps. Your spirits are the candles of the Lord! And remember that your bodies are God's temples. You must keep your lamps burning at all times. *Prayer* keeps it lit!

When you have problems—pray! When you do not have problems—pray! Do not run away from God when it gets difficult—Run to Him. Even if you are hurting and do not have the words to say, just cry out to Him in His presence. He is always waiting with open arms to embrace you, because He loves you with an everlasting Love! Never, Never, Never shut the door on the Lord. When He knocks on your door open it quickly and let Him in. What is He doing now? Praying for you and me—pray, pray, and keep on praying!

<u>Epilogue</u>

Just as a natural pearl is not formed overnight—a princess of God is not formed overnight. These princesses are very valuable to God and He desires to keep them close to His heart. Christ has to be formed inside of their hearts if they are willing. He is indeed a gentleman and will not force Himself on anyone. We all need Him to be our Keeper!

Perhaps you may still be wondering, "How in the world am I going to stay pure?" I am very glad you asked that question! We learned that the Word of God purifies, right? All I can do sister…is give you more of the Word! It may seem trite to you now, if you apply it—it could save your life! Please read this passage with a willingness to change and an open heart in 1 Peter 1:13-25(NIV). I believe it summarizes what we desire to achieve in our walk of purity.

Be Holy

Therefore, with minds that are alert and fully sober, set your hope on the grace to be brought to you when Jesus Christ is revealed at his coming. As obedient children, do not conform to the evil desires you had when you lived in ignorance. But just as he who called you is holy, so be holy in all you do; for it is written: "Be holy, because I am holy."

Since you call on a Father who judges each person's work impartially, live out your time as foreigners here in reverent fear. For you know that it was not with perishable things such as silver or gold that you were redeemed from the empty way of life handed down to you from your ancestors, but with the precious blood of Christ, a lamb without blemish or defect. He was chosen before the creation of the world, but was revealed in these last times for your sake. Through him you believe in God, who raised him from the dead and glorified him, and so your faith and hope are in God.

Now that you have purified yourselves by obeying the truth so that you have sincere love for each other, love one another deeply, from the heart. For you have been born again, not of perishable seed, but of imperishable, through the living and enduring word of God. For, 'All people are like grass, and all their glory is like the flowers of the field; the grass withers and the flowers fall, but the word of the Lord endures forever.' And this is the word that was preached.

We are still human and sometimes a particle or dirt will creep into our bodies. This is where we have to depend on Holy Spirit daily to purify us. Sometimes it helps to have a visual of seeing sin leave our lives. Therefore, I suggest a "Fire Ceremony!"

Some may not believe it takes all of this; but if you feel this will help—do it. You can use any method that is appropriate for you or your group. I believe this is key before entering the Ceremony of Purity with your father, mother, siblings, and family!

There was a time in history where men and women wore chastity belts. We do not use this practice today. However, I have heard of ladies pinning pieces of paper to their bras and panties. If you are having a challenge with sexual thoughts, it may help to write the Scripture on the paper and pin it to your underwear. It certainly could not hurt you—besides no one will see it but you, right?

(Warning: please use safety pins and not straight pins.)

Practicing the presence of God and getting the Word of God in your heart is your greatest offensive weapon. Prayer is an intricate part of our relationship with God. Personally, I would rather not live if I could not hear His sweet voice. It is my only way to communicate with my Creator. It is so comforting to know that I can always go back to my Creator for anything. Especially, when I get into a jam...I know He is waiting to show me great and mighty things when I show up to pray!

Say yes to Jesus and enter into a covenant with Him that you will not regret. He wants to be formed inside of you. You are a Pearl of great value with Him living inside. He can and will sustain you until you have reached maturity. At that time, He will have prepared your groom for you...His Princess!

Bibliography

Vine's Expository Dictionary of Old and New Testament Words, Copyright 1981 by Fleming H. Revell Company.

Ever Increasing Faith by Smith Wigglesworth, First published 1924 — Public Domain, This edition – Copyright 2012 Jawbone Digital.

Letters from God, Copyright 2011 Ivan Tait, Dunamis Holdings, Publishing, Austin, TX 78758

Here I am to Worship, Copyright 2014 CCLI, Inc., Tim Hughes album, Here I am to Worship.

Wikipedia, the free encyclopedia.

The Importance of Effective Communication, Edward G. Wertheim, Ph.D., 2008.

Prayers that Avail Much — Volume II, Copyright 1989 by Word Ministries, Inc., Germaine Copeland.

Glossary

1. **admonish**: to give friendly earnest advice or encouragement to

2. **analogous**: showing an analogy or a likeness that permits one to draw an analogy

3. **characteristic**: a distinguishing trait, quality, or property

4. **chastity**: the quality or state of being chaste: as in purity in conduct and intention, restraint and simplicity in design or expression; personal integrity

5. **communication**: a process by which information is exchanged between individuals through a common system of symbols, signs, or behavior <the function of pheromones in insect *communication*>; *also* : exchange of information

6. **concept**: something conceived in the mind : thought, notion: an abstract or generic idea generalized from particular instances

7. **concupiscence**: strong desire

8. **confom**: to be similar or identical

9. **contaminate**: to soil, stain, corrupt, or infect by contact or association

10. **covenant**: a written agreement or promise usually under seal between two or more parties especially for the performance of some action

11. **covetousness**: having a craving for possession

12. **deceitful**: not honest

13. **embrace**: to clasp in the arms : hug

14. **encounter**: to come upon face-to-face

15. **endeavor**: to strive to achieve or reach

16. **entwine**: to twine together or around

17. **establish**: to make firm or stable

18. **etiquette**: the conduct or procedure required by good breeding or prescribed by authority to be observed in social or official life

19. **exalt**: to elevate by praise or in estimation : glorify

20. **expound**: to explain by setting forth in careful

and often elaborate detail

21. **handmaiden**: a personal maid or female servant

22. **holiness**: the quality or state of being holy

23. **humility**: the quality or state of being humble

24. **idolatry**: the worship of a physical object as a god

25. **modesty**: propriety in dress, speech, or conduct

26. **mortify**: to destroy the strength, vitality, or functioning of

27. **obstacle**: something that impedes progress or achievement

28. **oyster**: any of various marine bivalve mollusks (family Ostreidae) that have a rough irregular shell closed by a single adductor muscle and include commercially important shellfish

29. **perishable**: liable to spoil or decay

30. **persecute**: to harass or punish in a manner designed to injure, grieve,

or afflict; *specifically* : to cause to suffer because of belief

31. **persistent**: continuing without change in function or structure

32. **posture**: the position or bearing of the body whether characteristic or assumed for a special purpose <erect *posture*>; a conscious mental or outward behavioral attitude

33. **prohibit**: to prevent from doing something

34. **purify**: to make pure: as, to clear from material defilement or imperfection, to free from guilt or moral or ceremonial blemish

35. **redeem**: to get or win back, to free from the consequences of sin

36. **reverence**: honor or respect felt or shown : deference; *especially* : profound adoring awed respect,

37. **sacred**: dedicated or set apart for the service or worship of a deity,

38. **salvation**: deliverance from the power and effects of sin

39. **sanctuary**: a consecrated place: as

the ancient Hebrew temple at Jerusalem
or its holy of holies

40. **society**: a community, nation, or broad
grouping of people having common
traditions, institutions, and collective
activities and interests

41. **submission**: an act of submitting to the
authority or control of another

42. **sustain**: to give support or relief to

43. **tenacity**: the quality or state of being
tenacious

44. **tenacious**: persistent in maintaining, adhering
to, or seeking something valued or desired

45. **trespass**: an unlawful act committed on the
person, property, or rights of another;
especially : a wrongful entry on real
property

46. **validate**: to recognize, establish, or illustrate
the worthiness or legitimacy of

47. **wither**: to become dry and sapless; *especially* :
to shrivel from or as if from loss of bodily
moisture

(All definitions taken from Merriam-Webster Online Dictionary)

My Journal

Every lady is a woman
but every woman is not a lady.